HUBBLE SPACE TELESCOPE

PHOTOGRAPHING THE UNIVERSE

By John Hamilton

A&D Xtreme
An imprint of Abdo Publishing | abdopublishing.com

Editor: Sue Hamilton
Graphic Design: Sue Hamilton
Cover Design: Candice Keimig
Cover Photo: iStock
Interior Photos: All photos NASA, except pg 11-Princeton University/Denise Applewhite and pg 29-Northrop Grumman.

Websites
To learn more about Xtreme Spacecraft, visit abdobooklinks.com. These links are routinely monitored and updated to provide the most current information available.

Publisher's Cataloging-in-Publication Data

Names: Hamilton, John, author.
Title: Hubble Space Telescope: photographing the universe / by John Hamilton.
Other titles: Photographing the universe
Description: Minneapolis, MN : Abdo Publishing, 2018. | Series: Xtreme spacecraft | Includes index.
Identifiers: LCCN 2016962229 | ISBN 9781532110122 (lib. bdg.) | ISBN 9781680787979 (ebook)
Subjects: LCSH: Hubbel Space Telescope (Spacecraft)--Juvenile literature. | Space telescopes--Exploration--Juvenile literature. | Outer space--Exploration--Juvenile literature. | Telescopes--Juvenile literature.
Classification: DDC 522--dc23
LC record available at http://lccn.loc.gov/2016962229

CONTENTS

PHOTOGRAPHING THE UNIVERSE

The Earth is always bathed in the light of distant stars. The light may take millions of years to reach us. But at the last moment, it must pass through Earth's thick atmosphere before it can be seen. Details become blurry. Stars appear to twinkle because of pockets of cold and warm air.

To make star gazing clearer, in 1990 NASA launched the Hubble Space Telescope (HST). It is an enormous observatory in orbit far above the Earth.

The Hubble Space Telescope can see 10 times farther than most telescopes on Earth. It detects objects that are one billion times dimmer than what can be seen by the human eye.

Whirlpool
Galaxy

After more than 25 years in orbit, it has made over 1.3 million observations. Hubble has changed our understanding of how the universe works.

The Pillars of Creation, part of M16, the Eagle Nebula, is one of the most popular images ever taken by Hubble. Gas clouds and dust glow from the radiation of young stars.

Glowing dust and gas make up part of the Orion Nebula. Astronomers combined 520 Hubble images to make this picture, which contains more than 3,000 stars. The Orion Nebula is 1,500 light years from Earth.

PLANNING AND BUILDING

Early telescopes were launched into space from the late 1940s to the early 1970s. They were built to detect ultraviolet light and x-rays, and did not last long.

NASA's Orbiting Astronomical Observatory Program launched four orbiting telescopes from 1966 to 1972. The OAOs were designed to show scientists the benefits of these devices. Only two OAOs successfully reached low Earth orbit. OAO-2's mission went from 1968 to 1973. OAO-3 operated from 1972 to 1981.

Astronomer Lyman Spitzer convinced the United States government to launch a large telescope that would work with visible light. That project became the Hubble Space Telescope.

Lyman Spitzer

NASA began building the Hubble Space Telescope in 1978. The European Space Agency provided solar cells and some science instruments. There were many delays in putting together the spacecraft. One of the most difficult pieces to build was Hubble's main mirror. It is 94.5 inches (240 cm) in diameter. Its curved, reflective surface had to be almost completely smooth and perfectly angled.

XTREME FACT – *The Hubble Space Telescope is the size of a large school bus. It is about 44 feet (13 m) long, has a maximum diameter of 14 feet (4 m), and weighs 27,000 pounds (12,247 kg).*

Technicians inspect the main mirror of the HST in 1982.

LAUNCH

After all its construction delays, Hubble was scheduled to launch in October 1986.

However, on January 28, 1986, the space shuttle *Challenger* exploded. The disaster grounded all shuttle flights for more than two years.

Challenger tragically exploded seconds into its 10th mission.

Hubble was rescheduled. Finally, on A_____ 1990, the space telescope was sent ____ orbit aboard space shuttle _Discovery_.

Hubble was released from the payload bay of space shuttle _Discovery_ on April 25, 1990. Today, HST orbits about 340 miles (547 km) above Earth. Traveling at 17,398 miles per hour (28,000 kph), it takes just 95 minutes to circle the planet.

IMAGING

Hubble is shaped like a hollow tube. Starlight enters one end and strikes the telescope's main mirror on the other side. The light is reflected into a smaller, secondary mirror. It then travels through a hole in the center of the main mirror.

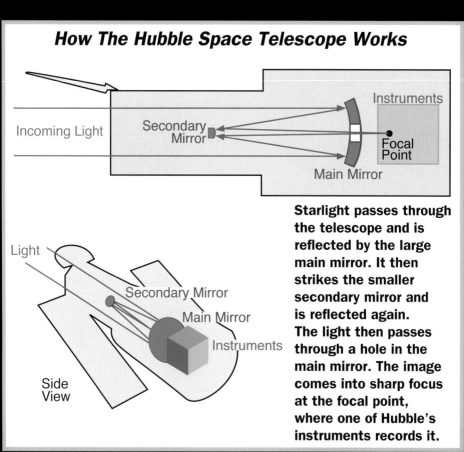

How The Hubble Space Telescope Works

Incoming Light

Secondary Mirror

Instruments

Focal Point

Main Mirror

Light

Secondary Mirror

Main Mirror

Instruments

Side View

Starlight passes through the telescope and is reflected by the large main mirror. It then strikes the smaller secondary mirror and is reflected again. The light then passes through a hole in the main mirror. The image comes into sharp focus at the focal point, where one of Hubble's instruments records it.

Several instruments capture the light. It is converted into images, much like a digital camera. Telescopes that use these kind of reflecting mirrors are called Cassegrains.

A photo of spiral galaxy NGC 6782 taken with Hubble's ultraviolet light camera.

XTREME FACT – Besides visible light, Hubble can also detect objects in ultraviolet (UV) and near-infrared wavelengths. (Earth's atmosphere blocks UV light.) By using infrared instruments, the space telescope can "see" objects that are hidden behind dust and gas clouds.

SERVICE MISSIONS

When Hubble first began sending images home to Earth, NASA scientists discovered a big problem. The images were fuzzy. The main mirror was flawed. The $1.5 billion telescope could not focus correctly. In 1993, astronauts from the space shuttle *Endeavour* corrected the flawed mirror by adding special electronics. It was like putting a contact lens on Hubble's big eye. The images were now perfectly sharp, and astronomers eagerly began exploring the heavens.

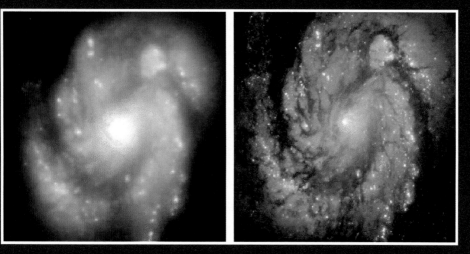

Photos of spiral galaxy M100 before and after HST was repaired in 1993.

Astronauts F. Story Musgrave (on the robotic arm) and Jeffrey Hoffman (payload bay) perform Hubble's first servicing mission in 1993. HST was designed to be repaired and maintained by astronauts. From 1993 to 2009, there were five service missions to the space telescope. Space shuttle crews replaced worn or outdated gyroscopes, cameras, batteries, computers, and solar arrays.

The complex structure of the Butterfly Nebula was created by a superhot dying star ejecting gas and dust. Its "wingspan" is more than three light years across. It is about 4,000 light years away, in the constellation Scorpio's stinger.

A barred spiral galaxy called NGC 6217 is about 60 million light years from Earth. It is in the constellation of Ursa Minor.

POWER AND COMMUNICATIONS

Hubble gets its power from sunlight. Two solar arrays on either side of the telescope convert light into electricity. When Hubble's orbit takes it through Earth's shadow, rechargeable batteries provide power.

XTREME FACT – Hubble communicates using two antennas. They send digital signals to satellites. The satellites then relay the data to large antennas in White Sands, New Mexico.

Hubble needs about 150 watts of energy to operate—about the same as two household light bulbs. Hubble's computers, gyroscopes, and guidance sensors keep it extremely stable. When taking pictures, its aim moves less than the width of a hair.

PARTS OF THE HUBBLE SPACE TELESCOPE

Main Mirror
is 7.9 feet (2.4 m) in diameter. It collects light from the telescope's targets and reflects it to the secondary mirror.

Fine Guidance Sensors (FGS)
point and lock the telescope on target.

Secondary Mirror is 12 inches (30.5 cm) in diameter. It reflects the light back through a hole in the main mirror and into the instruments.

Aperture Door can close to keep light from the Sun from entering and damaging the telescope.

Communication Antennas are usually extended, but are shown in the diagram in their down, or "berthed," positions.

Solar Panels provide enough power for all the science instruments to operate at the same time.

Reaction Wheels are used to move, or "reorient," the telescope.

Support Systems such as computers, gyroscopes, batteries, and other electronics are stored in these areas.

DISCOVERIES

The Hubble Space Telescope has taken thousands of beautiful, razor-sharp pictures of stars, planets, nebulae, and galaxies. It has helped astronomers understand how galaxies are created. It has revealed the age of the universe (the best estimate is about 13.8 billion years).

Ring Nebula Surrounds Star WR 124

Eagle Nebula

Jupiter

The Hubble Ultra Deep Field photographs captured images of the farthest galaxies ever seen. Astronomers will study Hubble's discoveries for many years as they try to unravel the mysteries of the universe.

This amazing Hubble Ultra Deep Field image shows thousands of galaxies in various ages, sizes, shapes, and colors.

XTREME FACT – *Hubble had its last servicing mission in 2009. The space telescope is currently operating very well. It will continue to be used by astronomers until its parts wear out or malfunction.*

OTHER SPACE TELESCOPES

NASA's Great Observatories Program has so far launched four space-based telescopes into orbit, including Hubble.

The Compton Gamma Ray Observatory was launched in 1991 and operated until 2000. The Chandra X-ray Observatory was launched in 1999. The Spitzer Space Telescope was launched in 2003.

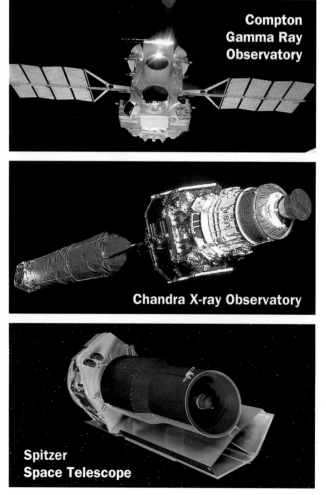

Compton Gamma Ray Observatory

Chandra X-ray Observatory

Spitzer Space Telescope

The James Webb Space Telescope (JWST) is scheduled to launch in 2018. It will be stationed about one million miles (1.6 million km) from Earth. Its infrared imaging system will reveal objects hidden behind clouds of dust and gas. It will also search for exoplanets orbiting distant stars.

James Webb
Space Telescope

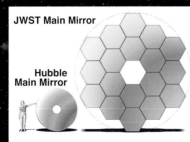

JWST Main Mirror

Hubble
Main Mirror

The James Webb Space Telescope's main mirror is over 21 feet (6.4 m) in diameter, compared to Hubble's 7.9 feet (2.4 m). The larger mirror, combined with the telescope's infrared sensors, will allow it to take sharp images of objects on the very edge of the known universe.

GLOSSARY

European Space Agency (ESA)
A space agency, like NASA, that builds and flies spacecraft that explore the solar system. Its headquarters is in Paris, France. As of 2017, there are 22 countries that are members of the ESA.

Exoplanet
A planet that orbits a distant star instead of the Sun. Astronomers have identified thousands of exoplanets in our galaxy. Some may have the right conditions to support life.

Expanding Universe
Astronomers have discovered that our universe is expanding. The speed of this expansion (its rate) is increasing. An expanding, or stretching, universe is difficult to understand. Think of a loaf of bread dough embedded with raisins. The dough represents space, and the raisins represent galaxies. As the bread bakes, it expands. The raisins don't move through the dough, but they still move apart from each other. It is similar to how our universe is expanding.

Gyroscope
A mechanical device often used in aircraft and spacecraft that provide stability and navigation.

LIGHT YEAR

A unit of distance. It is the distance that light travels in one year. Light travels about 186,000 miles (299,338 km) per second. That is about 7.5 times around Earth's equator. In one year, light travels almost 6 trillion miles (9.6 trillion km). The nearest star to Earth (other than the Sun) is Proxima Centauri. It is 4.24 light years away.

NATIONAL AERONAUTICS AND SPACE ADMINISTRATION (NASA)

A United States government space agency started in 1958. NASA's goals include space exploration, as well as increasing people's understanding of Earth, our solar system, and the universe.

NEBULA

A cloud of dust in space, plus a mix of hydrogen and helium gas. It resembles a giant cloud. In fact, nebula is the Latin word for cloud. Nebulae are where stars often form.

ORBIT

The circular path a moon or spacecraft makes when traveling around a planet or other large celestial body.

INDEX